God Renews Our
Relationships
With Others

God Renews Our
Relationships
With Others

Volume 3

By
Farley Dunn

THIS IS A MYCHURCHNOTES.NET BOOK

PUBLISHED BY MYCHURCHNOTES.NET
AND THREE SKILLET PUBLISHING
(www.ThreeSkilletPublishing.com)

COPYRIGHT © 2017 BY FARLEY DUNN

www.MyChurchNotes.net

God Renews Our Relationships with Others/Farley Dunn
1st ed.

Vol. 3

This is an original work created by
Farley Dunn for the website MyChurchNotes.net.

All rights reserved.

ISBN: 978-1-943189-47-2

Non-public domain scripture quotations are from The Holy Bible, English Standard Version® (ESV®), copyright © 2001 by Crossway, a publishing ministry of Good News Publishers. Used by permission. All rights reserved.

Dedication

For Bob . . .

. . . who came into our lives at just the right time and gave us a new focus on what's important.

MyChurchNotes.net

Table of Contents

Becoming What God Wants Us to Be	19
Finding Beauty in the Wildest Rose	25
Getting Excited	31
God's Crystal River	37
Greeting the Fool	43
Harnessed for the Lord's Work	49
Lifted Up by Love	55
Living Up to Our Aspirations	61
Our Salvation Proof	67
Our Standing Stone	73
Our Unexpected Happiness	79
Our Windowglass Wardrobe	85
Paper Chain Christianity	91
Proof of Our Devotion	97
Sharing Our Loaves and Fishes	103
Shearing Our Sheep	109
Stitched with the Thread of Christ	115
Taking One for the Team	119
Taking Our Hand off the Sword	125
The Bricks We Stand On	131
The Helpful Nephew	137
The Sons of Thunder	143
The Value of a Little Man	149
The Yin Pollutes the Yang	155
Threading the Needle of Christ	161
Unimportant Matters	167
Coming to Christ in Three Easy Steps	171

Introduction

We never know the importance we have in others' lives.

It's only in the after-moments, when we can see things with hindsight, that our true significance comes into perspective. A story told, or a letter written, reveals emotions (for good or for bad) that have affected those we've been in contact with over the days of our lives.

What legacy do we want to leave? What's the impact on the lives of those we've lived among that we want them to remember? Kindness cannot be a one-off experience. We can't choose to be moody today and cheerful tomorrow, because those who cross our path will remember the moody as well as the cheerful. We can't simply erase one with the other. We must live each day as if it's the only one that matters, because to the people we see between that sunrise and sunset, it's the only day we have to offer. What we do in those hours is what they'll remember for the rest of their lives.

"God's Crystal River" tells us that God's purity is revealed in our love for others.

"Harnessed for the Lord's Work" reveals that love, not harsh words or criticism, is how we bring others to Christ.

"The Sons of Thunder" says we can be superheroes when we step out in the authority of our Lord and Savior.

Plus enjoy 23 more inspirational essays to help you lead a fulfilling Christian life.

Every day we touch the lives of the people around us. Every day, we need to let the Lord reveal his compassion through our actions toward them.

Farley Dunn

Light Bulb Moment

Let's step up for God, and become what God wants us to be.

Becoming What God Wants Us to Be

(Fair Play)

VISIT AN old-world market. Haggling is the name of the game. I offer this, you counter my offer. We swing our perceived value of the merchandise back and forth until we come to an agreement.

I only want to pay what I feel comfortable with. You have to sell it for enough to cover your expenses.

Who wants to take a loss, either in selling it for less than it costs to produce, or in paying more than you can recoup when you resell?

Some manufacturers consider a loss a good deal. Microsoft famously sells its gaming units for less than they cost to produce, knowing it will more than remake its money on the games it sells. The software giant considers its trade-off fair play. Everyone wins, either in good value for a good product, or in profits fairly earned.

What about unfair play? We're forced to borrow money at exorbitant rates; our company is driven into the ground to be snapped up and resold by a larger company; or we're hoodwinked into purchasing poor investments so someone else can become rich?

Habakkuk 2:7 tells us:

> "Shall they not rise up suddenly that shall bite you, and awake that shall vex you, and you shall be for [riches] unto them?"

The prophet refers to the Chaldeans in this passage, but his words are aimed at any people who oppress another. Do we borrow our neighbor's mower and return it with the gas tank empty? How about the pizza delivery guy? Do we tip him enough to make his job worthwhile? Then there's our children. Do we hug them as we correct them? They only grow up once. Shouldn't they be given the best experience possible?

Habakkuk's words tell us that the head of the snake will become the tail. What we do will come back on us. If we mistreat others, they will become vengeful towards us.

Jesus' words tell us to do unto others as we would have them do unto us. If we want them to tell us good morning, we need to say it first. If we want a hug, hug first. Giving good gifts? Be first in line.

Treating others well is always a good investment. It's fair play, because what we give out is what comes our way, time and time again.

Let's step up for God, and become what God wants us to be.

Light Bulb Moment

Jesus enjoyed the roses, and he never let the thorns get in his way.

Finding Beauty in the Wildest Rose

ROSES HAVE thorns, yet we don't chuck the bushes from our gardens. The blooms are too magnificent. Instead, we find a way to handle the rosebushes in such a way that the thorns do as little damage to us as possible.

At times thick gloves are all we need. The thorns can prick us, but we don't feel them. However, the gloves take away part of the enjoyment, because we can't stroke the blooms to feel their magnificence.

Other times we choose to enjoy the roses from a distance, giving them a location at the furthest edges of the lawn. There, no one has to touch them. Yet, a rose is best enjoyed up close, and we lose much of our enjoyment in the beauty and aroma of the blooms.

There are thornless varieties out there. These, though, need to be babied, and somehow, it seems their blooms are never as bright or full as those that cut us when we handle them carelessly.

Coastal Maine is renowned for the beauty of its wild roses. They bloom in exuberant abundance in the summer months. They don't have to be cultivated, no one coddles them, and their aroma is a heady sensation of outlandish proportions. Bring a bouquet into the house, and every time we walk near, we'll catch a whiff of the wonderful outdoors.

Those Maine roses? They are covered with thorns. Fall into a patch, and we'll be bloodied from head to toe.

Yet their beauty will remain undiminished.

Jesus walked among the wild roses in his time on earth. We, mankind, were the magnificent blossoms he cherished, yet our words of unbelief were the thorns he was forced to endure. Yet, when he chose to live among us, he threw away his gloves, because he wanted to feel our beauty skin to skin. He kept us close, because that's how much he enjoyed us. And thornless? Maybe the angels, but not heady and arrogant humanity.

Jesus loved the wild roses, those people who struggled with life, who smelled most sweetly when blooming in a profusion of thorns.

Psalms 119:83 tells us:

> "For I have become like a wineskin in the smoke, yet I have not forgotten your statutes."

The references in this verse may be archaic, but the meaning is not. A wineskin among the flames dries out and is useless. The same wineskin thrown into the thorns will be punctured and left unable to serve its intended purpose.

The second half of the verse is what's important. When we remember we are God's creation, then even in the turmoil of our earthly lives, we will continue to find the beauty in one another that Christ saw in us.

What statute is so important that we cannot afford to forget it? Look to John 13:34:

> "A new commandment I give to you, that you love one another."

Jesus did it. If we follow his example, we will love one another, and we will find the beauty of the wild Maine rose in every person we meet. We will handle them with care, for we will find the blooms to be far more important than the thorns we have to avoid. We will be like Jesus, even when the thorns pierce us and leave blood on our skin.

Love one another. That's from Jesus. It's the only way to live.

Jesus enjoyed the roses, and he never let the thorns get in his way.

Light Bulb Moment

When we are enthused with Christ, it will spread to those around us.

Getting Excited

MOST OF US don't study quantum mechanics. The reality of it, however, is all around us. We can't escape quantum mechanics if we try.

Hold someone's hand. Are they alive and warm to the touch? If so, we've just experienced excitation, a basic concept in quantum mechanics. When an atom moves faster than the atoms around it, it has greater heat. When it moves fast enough, it feels warm to us.

We seek warmth, because we must have it in order to survive.

How can we find warmth in our walk with our Lord? We have a good start in Isaiah 61:10:

> "I will greatly rejoice in the Lord; my soul shall exult in my God, for he has clothed me with the garments of salvation; he has covered me with

the robe of righteousness, as a bridegroom decks himself like a priest with a beautiful headdress, and as a bride adorns herself with her jewels."

When we get excited in the Lord, we create a little pocket of spiritual warmth. We bump into other people's spiritual atoms, and they begin to move, also. Then they begin to bump into others, and the warmth grows until it becomes a mighty flame, ripping across the land, and igniting spirits for the Lord all across the world.

In that moment, we've become a study in quantum mechanics. We've raised ourselves to an excited state, given ourselves more energy than those around us, and begun to affect those we come into contact with.

Quantum mechanics also says the lifetime of our excited state is usually short. Why? The energy we give off leaves us drained. We constantly have to find some way to give ourselves extra energy.

We get our extra energy by studying the Word and praising our glorious Heavenly Father. When we keep that up, we will remain excited about him all the time. The excitation of being involved with the Almighty God of all Creation is something a Christian must have in order to survive.

When we are enthused with Christ, it will spread to those around us.

Light Bulb Moment

It's the purity of love that God wants the world to see in us, not the effluent of a life lived in the cacophony of blessings we sometimes see as our due.

God's Crystal River

THE MOUNTAINS of western Massachusetts are littered with waterfalls. Most flow year round, and they are beautiful.

However, let the rains come, and they become gushing behemoths that will awe and amaze everyone who approaches their thundering majesty.

One of these is Campbell Falls. Located on the border of Massachusetts and Connecticut, the park in which they are located drapes across the state border. The falls tumble down Massachusetts' granite boulders, but the stream continues on to water the Connecticut countryside.

In late September 2015, a massive series of storms swept across New England, breaking a months-long dry spell. The pristine water tumbling down the falls became a torrent of brown effluent.

Yet, only several hundred feet away, the flow swept into Connecticut, crystal clear and beautiful.

When we pray for God's outflowing blessings, sometimes it's the same. Along with the desired bounty we beseech from the Lord comes the dirt and silt stirred up by the torrent of blessings he tumbles upon our heads. Others see our blessings, and greed is stirred. Hidden sins are brought to light. Even desires we thought long submerged suddenly erupt in their verdant majesty, crowding out the beauty of God in our lives.

We get what we asked for, but it doesn't come without a price.

The water flowing across Campbell Falls becomes pure before reaching Connecticut because of the rocks across which it tumbles and the still pools along the way. All the silt stirred up by the rush of water over the falls becomes of no consequence if we just give it enough time to purify itself through God's natural processes.

Revelation 22:1-2 tells us:

> "Then the angel showed me the river of the water of life, bright as crystal, flowing from the throne of God and of the Lamb through the

middle of the street of the city; also, on either side of the river, the tree of life with its twelve kinds of fruit, yielding its fruit each month. The leaves of the tree were for the healing of the nations."

When we let Christ sift our lives, our blessings will abound, and the world will slough away, cleansed by his blood. We will become the healing of the nations, part of God's crystal river, a blessing for those around us each and every day.

It's the purity of love that God wants the world to see in us, not the effluent of a life lived in the cacophony of blessings we sometimes see as our due.

G ood manners bring God's blessings on everything we do.

Greeting the Fool

WE ALL KNOW at least one fool, that person who never learns from his mistakes, but continues to do the same thing over and over, expecting a different outcome if he just keeps on trying.

"The old college try," he laughs, as he remarries for the fourth time.

Or what about the gal who buys her third or fifth used car, exclaiming how sporty it looks, only to find it in the shop the week after she brings it home.

Other people manage to find more serious ways to show their foolishness. No more is the bankruptcy settled than the credit card debt begins to rise once more. Or the day after rehab is over, he scores another "hit," wanting to feel that "high" once again.

We want to shunt these fools aside and get on with

our lives, but is that the Godly thing to do?

In 1 Samuel 25, we read of Nabal, an exceedingly rich man from Maon, with 3,000 sheep and 1,000 goats. He was of the house of Caleb, but his spirit and faith had diverged onto the paths of foolishness.

Samuel the prophet had just died at the age of 98, and Saul no longer knew any restraints. David, not yet king, was on the run for his life. He came upon Nabal shearing his sheep.

Verse 5 tells us: "David sent out ten young men, and David said unto the young men, Get you up to Carmel, and go to Nabal, and greet him in my name."

The situation quickly spirals downhill, for Nabal fully plays the part of the fool. He insults David, insinuating he is little more than an escaped slave who should run back to Saul, his master.

It was nearly the death of Nabal, and it would have been if not for the wisdom of Nabal's wife, Abigail, who steps in as mediator and peacemaker.

David acted in full propriety, and when the fool was foolish in return, God ordered the situation to David's benefit. In short order, Nabal died a natural death, and all Nabal's possessions, including his wife, were given into David's hands.

Even the foolish person deserves to be treated with respect. God demands that of us. Their judgment is in God's hands, not ours. He will take care of them in his own good time.

Good manners bring God's blessings on everything we do.

Light Bulb Moment

When we harness love, we are fully prepared to go unto the world and present to them the message of salvation.

Harnessed for the Lord's Work

SOMETIMES WE want to jump in with both feet. Go whole hog. Give it both barrels. Head over heels.

We mean we plan to give 100% of everything we've got, so that the job gets done to the best of our ability. What could be wrong with that?

Several years ago a man and a woman showed up at the emergency room. She was fine. He was beat to a pulp. She explained the care her husband had put into the new fireplace in the basement. He'd studied mortar ratios, bricklaying, and even the best firebrick to install in the firebox. Then, finished, he'd immediately started a fire.

The fireplace exploded around him. The water in the uncured mortar turned into steam and destroyed everything the man had created. He missed one detail, and that undid everything he'd built.

Christians can be like that sometimes. God gives us an instruction book that explains every step of our salvation. However, we're filled with so much enthusiasm that we just jump in and light the fire of God under newly minted believers. Then we don't understand when they disintegrate around us, shattered by the heat of something they weren't prepared for.

Psalm 32:9 tells us:

> "Be not as the horse, or as the mule, which have no understanding: whose mouth must be held in with bit and bridle, lest they come near unto you."

We've seen this Christian. If we're shopping in the wrong store, or visiting with the wrong person, the backlash of their rebuke curls the hair on our head. Heaven forbid we miss Wednesday night prayer or mow our yard in a sleeveless shirt. We'll find our name on someone's prayer list.

Sometimes we need to let God's Word harness our mouths so that what we say doesn't harm other people. What did Jesus say in John 13:35?

> "By this shall all men know that you are my dis-

ciples, if you have love one to another."

Love, not harsh words, criticism, or putting their names on yet another prayer list. How can we show love one to another? Kind words, patience, and understanding are a good start. When we do those things, we've changed from a mule with no understanding, to a follower of Christ who can cast the bit and bridle away. We will have control of our tongues, and no one will need fear anything we have to say.

When we harness love, we are fully prepared to go unto the world and present to them the message of salvation.

Light Bulb Moment

When we truly love, we step out as Christ did and show that love to others.

Lifted Up by Love

SOMETIMES WE get love wrong. We only see the emotion, and it's more than that. The most enduring love is an action, something we do that shows someone we care.

Love makes life better for those we care about. Let's look at five proofs.

Love Proof #1:

> Proverbs 22:15 tells us love helps us give direction to our children, keeping them from making foolish choices.
>
> Love isn't about always saying yes, but about saying let's discuss it.

Love Proof #2:

> Ephesians 2:8-9 says love is a gift, and we never have to earn it.

We endeavor to improve the lives of the ones we love because we love them, not because they can give us something in return.

Love Proof #3:

Hebrews 12:5-11 lets us know that love involves discipline.

If we love without correction, we become an enabler, allowing and supporting poor behaviors that become harmful to our loved ones.

Love Proof #4:

2 Timothy 3:16 reveals a plan for showing our love to others.

Love as only an emotion is hollow. The Bible gives us a plan for action so that others can see our love.

Love Proof #5:

Acts 4:12 gives us the ultimate love.

Christ loved us before we were born, and he knew we'd never know the extent of his compassion for us without putting action to his emotions. He came to earth, became a man, and gave his life for us in the most painful way possible. He did it to make life better for those he cared about.

Jesus came to improve the world in which we live.

Jesus' example is our example. If we truly love our fellow man, we must get out of our living rooms and show them. That's what love is all about, action, something we do that shows someone we care.

Bake a cake for a neighbor. Visit a coworker in the hospital. Offer to give someone a ride. Tell that grandson a little money is on the way. Teach a Sunday school class one weekend. Mow an elderly person's yard.

Put love into action, and the world will be lifted up by love.

When we truly love, we step out as Christ did and show that love to others.

Light Bulb Moment

When we stand for our commitments, we lift Jesus before the world.

Living Up to Our Aspirations

MAN UP.

What those two words really tell us is to hold ourselves to a standard. Don't lower the bar when the road we've chosen becomes difficult to walk.

We fall in love with the perfect person, and after we tie the knot, we begin to see the flaws that were invisible in our first flush of passion. Man up, dudes and chicks! Your commitment is still in play!

Our son sinks into drugs, and he wreaks havoc on our life. He steals from us, fractures our relationship with our spouse, and undermines us financially. We want him gone. We have to man up and maintain our commitment. We're the only hope he has.

Our pastor stumbles, and the church becomes divided. We tire of explaining why we continue worshipping at a flawed fellowship. We want to find a better church. Man up! Christ didn't cast aside sinners because they weren't perfect. He drew them in so he could minister unto them.

We have to be better than we are in order that others might see us living out the love of Christ to those around us.

1 Timothy 3:1-2 sets our goal, telling us that if we desire a high office in the Church, we must set our personal standards high and never falter.

Why? People are watching us. They expect more of us. Our failure will do more damage, because we're more visible.

Who watches our marriage fall apart and sees that hallowed institution as a joke and a sham?

Who watches us cast aside our children and decides he has no responsibility to his own?

Who watches us abandon our fellowship and decides church hopping is the way to search for spiritual truth?

We have to man up to our aspirations. Whether

marriage, children, or our chosen fellowship, when we make a commitment, it's long term. To cast it carelessly aside is to cause others to stumble on our fractured and broken standards.

Instead we must set the example that God's Word espouses. We must hold him high in everything we do.

When we stand for our commitments, we lift Jesus before the world.

Light Bulb Moment

When the world listens to us proclaim our love for Christ, they will look for proof in the love we show our fellow man.

Our Salvation Proof

WE'RE USED to providing proof.

Before computers became common in store check-out lanes, customers could pay with cash or checks. Anyone who wrote a check had to provide identification to prove they were who they said they were, often in the form of a driver's license or a credit card.

Online banking is no different. We have log-in IDs, but it's our password that gains us entrance, and that's only if we also know our special images or the answers to our security questions.

How many people today log in at work with their thumbprint? In public schools and other security-conscious jobs, the rate is growing exponentially.

The high-tech industry relies on voice technology and eye scanners. We want people to be who they say they are. No imposters are allowed.

How do we know the salvation brought by Jesus is the real thing? What proof do we have?

We find our answer in 1 Corinthians 11:25:

> "After the same manner also he took the cup, when he had supped, saying, This cup is the new testament in my blood: this do you, as oft as you drink it, in remembrance of me."

Jesus knew his manner of upcoming death. His blood would soon be shed for the salvation of the world, and his disciples would need a physical reminder to sustain them through the dark days ahead. He offered that proof in the cup of wine that represented his shed blood for the redemption of fallen humanity.

Where is our salvation proof today? What do we offer the world as an assurance that our claims of Christianity are real, that we are who we say we are?

Is it possible to prove we are who we say we are?

In John 15:12, Jesus tells us:

> "This is my commandment, that you love one

another, as I have loved you."

There it is, in a nutshell, the proof that we are followers of Christ. In that verse we find our log-in ID, our password, our special image, and all the answers to our security questions. It even contains our spiritual thumbprint.

Not even an eye scanner will have trouble recognizing who we are: children of the King.

Our love for those who walk at our side is our proof that we live in the salvation of Christ our King.

When the world listens to us proclaim our love for Christ, they will look for proof in the love we show our fellow man.

Light Bulb Moment

When we stand close to the Christians at our side, our shoulders will ensure no one ever falls away from the loving arms of Jesus.

Our Standing Stone

HOW DO WE not fall down?

Okay, that's an easy one. We place both feet on the floor and hold our back erect. But for some people, it's not so simple. A head injury can knock us for a permanent loop, and every time we get to our feet, the world swirls around us.

Other times, infections, medications, or low blood pressure can cause us to sway and topple.

Then there are muscular disorders and skeletal problems, such as arthritis. We fall down for all sorts of reasons.

One reason none of us can escape is age. As we grow more experienced in life, and we seem to gain control of our money, our emotions, and our empathy toward others, our body begins to give way, and we tumble to the ground more and more easily.

How can we be so surprised when a mature Christian occasionally tumbles away from Christ and has to be picked up, brushed off, and put on her feet again?

We need to be the buttress against which others may lean so that no one falls too far towards the ground. We need to be standing stones for our Christian brothers and sisters so that our weaknesses don't become our waywardness.

1 Timothy 3:15 tells us:

> "If I delay, you may know how one ought to behave in the household of God, which is the church of the living God, a pillar and buttress of the truth."

A pillar and a buttress of truth. A standing stone. A bulwark against which others can lean in their times of weakness, so they might stand again when they've regained their sense of balance.

The scripture goes on to tell us:

> "So then, brothers, stand firm and hold to the traditions that you were taught by us, either by our spoken word or by our letter."

If we decide to take our ease and lie down on the

job, we've failed our fellow Christians. It's in standing tall that we provide support for those who need us most.

The question becomes, How? How can we become that rigid tower, that walking stick, that steel walking aid that gets our brothers and sisters to the other side?

Let's think about what causes our balance problems. Almost every reason comes back to our ears. Our body relies on a series of tubes in our ears to keep us upright. That's right, our ears.

When we tell people words of support, we become their walking cane. When we listen to them pour out their hearts, we turn into a rigid tower. When we let them hear our spoken words of praise to our Holy Father in heaven, we are a standing stone against which they can lean in their time of weakness.

When we stand close to the Christians at our side, our shoulders will ensure no one ever falls away from the loving arms of Jesus.

Light Bulb Moment

We will find our happiness in Jesus through what we choose to do for others.

Our Unexpected Happiness

WE ALL WANT to be happy. Yet how do we find it? Is it packaged and on a shelf, ready to be parceled out to whoever needs it?

Scientific studies show us our happiness is determined by three things: genetics, material possessions, and personal choices. Half of whether we'll be happy or not is determined at birth. Some people are simply luckier than others. Ten percent comes from what we own. It follows that a person with a house and food to eat will be happier than a homeless person, but a mansion and haute cuisine don't increase happiness over the long term.

The other forty percent is up to us. How do we interact with others to increase our chances of being happy? It comes down to the dopamine in our brains. We get a dose every time our brain cells fire, so the more we *do*, and in the widest variety of ways possible, the happier we'll be. The biggest obstacle to happiness? Doing the same thing over and over in exactly the same way.

So why do we attend church each week, sing the same songs, pray the same prayers, and expect God to bring us happiness? That's forty percent of our chance for happiness lost right there. We need to shake things up. When we do, everything around us will seem to change.

Isaiah 55:13 tells us:

> "Instead of the thorn shall come up the cypress; instead of the brier shall come up the myrtle; and it shall make a name for the Lord, an everlasting sign that shall not be cut off."

Let's dance a jig to celebrate our happiness that comes from the Lord. More simply, we need to sit in a different pew at church. Change the numbers on our check before we drop it in the offering plate. Greet someone we haven't spoken to in the past two weeks. Volunteer to fill in as a Sunday school teacher for the next week.

When we use our forty percent wisely, we'll open our eyes in the mornings to find unexpected happiness there to greet us. It's ours for the asking. All we need to do is get out of our rut and into the worship of our Almighty God.

We will find our happiness in Jesus through what we choose to do for others.

Light Bulb Moment

When we wear Jesus, his presence outshines everything else in our life.

Our Windowglass Wardrobe

THE EMPEROR'S New Clothes is a child's story designed to illustrate the empty façade of vanity.

In the tale, two tailors pretend to possess a cloth that can only be seen by the most cultured eyes. Hence, if the emperor can't see the fabric, then he shouldn't be emperor. So, the emperor pretends, and so do his courtiers, royal hangers-on, and other court aficionados.

They all want to be seen as brilliant, and so they pretended to see something brilliant. Yet, that something is nothing at all. It's an empty promise that leads the emperor to walk about town clothed in nothing more than his underwear.

It's as if he clothed himself with windowglass, and let the whole world peer through to see what he thought was hidden.

Our spiritual lives are the same. We clothe ourselves in Sunday morning worship, Wednesday evening prayer, and visits to the sick. We put on modest clothing, strip our jewelry from our hands, and bind our hair to look properly religious.

It's all windowglass. What we are underneath is obvious to everyone we meet. They're not fooled, even if they pretend to see our manufactured godliness as the real deal.

Isaiah 3:18 tells us:

> "In that day the Lord will take away the finery of the anklets, the headbands, and the crescents."

This verse is pulled from a longer passage that decries Israel's dependence on anything other than God for her self-worth. What it tells us is that God will strip away anything false from his people, and they will be revealed as they really are. If they are idol-worshippers, their idols will be revealed. If they chase false sensuality, the nations will see. If high standing in the community drives them, their underpinnings will be taken away.

Only what is true will remain.

Who are we when exposed by our windowglass wardrobe? What truths come out about us?

Jesus gave us the ultimate wardrobe: Love your brothers as yourself.

Is that what people see in us? It's what forms our underwear, and through the windowglass of our pretentious Christianity, it's all the world will see even when we think we're dressed to the nines in the best we can manufacture.

When we wear Jesus, his presence outshines everything else in our life.

Light Bulb Moment

The true Christian experience is about holding hands and being the strength to others that they can't find on their own.

Paper Chain Christianity

PAPER CHAINS are fun to make. They're simple, they require little skill, and even children can do it.

Visit an elementary school classroom, and paper chains are de rigueur. They are part of the setting, either counting off days to something important, or showing levels of accomplishment for academic endeavors.

Being lightweight, paper chains can be stretched from point to point, crisscrossing the room, creating a swaying plethora of bright colors that dances with the movement of anyone who walks underneath.

Here's the downside of paper chains. Tear one, and the rest lose their interconnected strength. Oh, if we pull it from the end, the chain only grows smaller, but rip a link in the middle, and our plethora of dancing brilliance crashes to the floor.

We have to exercise care in our handling of our paper chains.

1 John 3:17 tells us:

> "But if anyone has the world's goods and sees his brother in need, yet closes his heart against him, how does God's love abide in him?"

This verse comes to us in four parts. Four paper chain links. Let's look at them one link at a time.

> "But if anyone has the world's goods . . ."

If God has blessed us with prosperity, then we have an obligation to our fellow believers. That's scriptural. Read it in black and white.

> ". . . and sees his brother in need . . ."

Not everyone has enough. There will be times our Christian brothers and sisters need our help to get by. It's that paper chain thing, each link supporting the one attached to it.

> ". . . yet closes his heart against him . . ."

This is the paper link carelessly torn and cast aside. How can the rest of the chain remain whole when one link falters in its duty?

". . . how does God's love abide in him?"

What is God's love? Compassion. Bearing all hurts. A level of goodness that is so out of the ordinary that it's not humanly possible for us to maintain it without the power of Christ in our lives.

Our Christian fellowship is a paper chain that depends on every link to cradle and support the links around it. When we exercise care in our handling of our relationships, we will be a swaying plethora of bright colors that shouts God's presence to anyone who happens by.

The true Christian experience is about holding hands and being the strength to others that they can't find on their own.

Light Bulb Moment

When we act out our love is when the world sees that our love for Christ is real.

Proof of Our Devotion

WE ALWAYS want proof.

Just go apply for a passport, if we doubt that. And it's not true just in legal matters. In relationships, we're always on the lookout for signals that we're the center of our partner's devotion. Eyes. Did he glance at that pretty girl? Cell phone. Who has she been calling? It's in the way he says "Good morning," and the enthusiasm of her kiss when he comes home from work.

Proof. It's plain and simple. We're all legal experts in this matter, detectives of a sort, able to root out the barest sign that something's amiss.

And when we overlook the clues? We're devastated. We feel our betrayal comes out of nowhere. We were blindsided, and we begin to search for what we hadn't even seen coming.

Why? We don't want to be betrayed again.

Some cynics doubt the truth of the Word. Jesus was just a man. The spirit of godliness came over him when John baptized him, and it left him on the cross. He was born human, and he died human, to be buried forever in the grave. He hasn't risen, and death claimed him for its own, just as it will each of us.

The Bible says differently, and we can find our proof between its covers.

James 2:18 tells us:

> "But someone will say, 'You have faith and I have works.' Show me your faith apart from your works, and I will show you my faith by my works."

What we do proves who we are. Just like with that passport. When we can pull out a valid birth certificate and picture ID, they support our claims of citizenship. We are who we say we are.

In love, the proof is in our actions. We hold the door, give the expected kiss, and our eyes sparkle with recognition each time we greet our partner. It's something the whole world can see.

How about Jesus? What's his proof? We find it in 1 John 3:16:

> "By this we know love, that he laid down his life for us, and we ought to lay down our lives for the brothers."

So, how can we prove our Christian love for our friends and families? The answer is in the same verse, that we ought to lay down our lives for our brothers.

We do this in rather more practical ways. We step in when our church members are in financial difficulties. We offer our support during times of emotional stress. Our time becomes theirs. We fill the gap when the church needs us, and in that action, we offer proof of who we are.

We are the followers of Christ. The proof of his divinity is found in an empty tomb. The proof of his love is seen in his death on the cross.

Our love toward our Christian companions is the proof of our devotion to him.

When we act out our love is when the world sees that our love for Christ is real.

Light Bulb Moment

When we offer our best to Jesus, he makes it greater than it was before.

Sharing Our Loaves and Fishes

EVERYONE HAS blessings of one sort or another.

Aunt Bessie may not have much money, but boy does her lemon pie beat any other dessert at the dinner table.

John down the street may be a single father, but his kids feel they are loved.

Sister Ruby may be bound to a wheel chair, but she can write checks to fund the Lord's work.

Everyone has felt the giving hand of God on his or her life, even if it sometimes feels otherwise. Each of us has something to offer those around us.

The boy in the story of the loaves and fishes didn't feel especially blessed. His mother had prepared him a sack lunch that day, and it was only thing he carried with him. Shoes? Bah! MP3 player? Not happening! He was probably wearing the only suit of clothes he owned, and it was coarse by today's standards.

Yet, the boy had something he could share, his loaves and fishes, and there was plenty to go around. The truth is found not in our abundance, but in sharing what little we possess.

Deuteronomy 14:29 gives us instructions on how to share our loaves and fishes.

> "And the Levite, (because he has no part nor inheritance with you,) and the stranger, and the fatherless, and the widow, which are within your gates, shall come, and shall eat and be satisfied; that the Lord your God may bless you in all the work of your hand which you do."

It doesn't matter if the hungry man is our brother. We are to feed him. According to this passage, because he is not our brother, we are under a greater obligation to feed him.

> . . . or love him.

> . . . or pay his bills.

> . . . or offer him a ride.

. . . or clothe him.

. . . or give him a job.

. . . or mow his yard.

. . . or pray for his soul.

. . . or forgive him.

Let's do what we can. Let's identify the loaves and fishes in our lunch sack, and let's offer our bounty to build up the lives of those around us.

When we offer our best to Jesus, he makes it greater than it was before.

Light Bulb Moment

When Jesus grows on us, he produces a harvest we can share with the world.

Shearing Our Sheep

SO, WHAT good are sheep?

The Bible references sheep frequently. Jesus is called the Good Shepherd . . . which makes us . . . wait for it . . . his flock, his sheep, the round, fluffy creatures that munch on grass and don't do much else.

No one has ever given a sheep a Rorschach inkblot test and commented, "Wow! I never knew sheep were so intelligent."

So, what good are sheep? The obvious answer is lamb chops and a nice wool cardigan. Right?

In truth, Jesus doesn't want our lamb chops. We're not much good to him sliced up and served on a plate, but our wool? That's an entirely different sweater.

Let's start with the quality of our wool.

2 Timothy 3:16 tells us how to ensure our wool is well maintained:

> "All Scripture is breathed out by God and profitable for teaching, for reproof, for correction, and for training in righteousness."

Matthew 16:18 describes how our wool can become a Kevlar lining:

> "And I tell you, you are Peter, and on this rock I will build my church, and the gates of hell shall not prevail against it."

1 Corinthians 9:5 lets us know two cardigans keep us warmer than one:

> "Do we not have the right to take along a believing wife, as do the other apostles and the brothers of the Lord and Cephas?"

Acts 20:28 is clear on our responsibility to the sheep around us:

> "Pay careful attention to yourselves and to all the flock, in which the Holy Spirit has made you overseers, to care for the church of God, which he obtained with his own blood."

Matthew 16:19 is wool on steroids:

> "I will give you the keys of the kingdom of heaven, and whatever you bind on earth shall be bound in heaven, and whatever you loose on earth shall be loosed in heaven."

Titus 1:5 gives our wool time to grow to fullness and maturity:

> "This is why I left you in Crete, so that you might put what remained into order, and appoint elders in every town as I directed you—"

2 Timothy 3:17 tells why we share our wool:

> "That the man of God may be competent, equipped for every good work."

Acts 17:11 illustrates the process for producing the best wool in the world:

> "Now these Jews were more noble than those in Thessalonica; they received the word with all eagerness, examining the Scriptures daily to see if these things were so."

So, what good are sheep? It's not about the lamb chops. It's about what we shear off. It's all about our wool: our love, deep compassion, a strident longing for the Word, and an ardent belief in doing good for our fellow man.

Who wouldn't want to be a sheep, one of the Jesus flock, anyway?

When Jesus grows on us, he produces a harvest we can share with the world.

Light Bulb Moment

When our life falls apart, Jesus is ready to put us back together.

Stitched with the Thread of Christ

IT'S A SOUND we dread. We sit or bend over, and the rending of fabric catches our ears.

Our clothing is damaged. We immediately search for a mirror, inspecting our garments to find the tear. Is it visible to others? Can they tell?

Next comes the repairs. Needle and thread? If it's available. However, a stapler, safety pin, or jacket might have to do. Anything, as long as we can make it through the day.

Humanity was rent in the Garden of Eden. Irreparably. We were sundered from the eternal presence of God by the wiles of the devil foisted on the trusting nature of God's creation.

Christ is our solution. Ezekiel 34:16 gives the words

of God as he speaks to his people:

> "I will seek that which was lost, and bring again that which was driven away, and will bind up that which was broken, and will strengthen that which was sick: but I will destroy the fat and the strong; I will feed them with Judgment."

This promise comes to us today through the person of Jesus of Nazareth. He is the thread that repairs the damage done in the Garden. He weaves us together into cloth stronger than it was before. He is our repair, our solution, and our everlasting hope of life renewed.

Further in the chapter, Ezekiel 34:22 sums up the powerful promise of God:

> "Therefore I will save my flock, and they shall no more be a prey; and I will judge between [them]."

We no longer need to feel lost. God's promise is already here. Christ is the thread of our renewal, and when we allow him into our hearts, he will stitch us into perfection, totally flawless in his name.

When our life falls apart, Jesus is ready to put us back together.

Our Christian walk is not about us. It's about all of us.

Taking One for the Team

HUMAN BEINGS work best in partnerships. Friendships, marriages, neighborhood watches, city governments, and on up the line are the lubricant that keeps our society running smoothly.

Striking out on our own scours away the oil of personal relationships, and the friction of daily life soon begins to burn bridges that can never be rebuilt.

Basketball is a good example. It's a team effort out there. A guard has to guard, but given an opening, the same guard has to be ready to step into any opening—and by the same measure, the rest of the team has to be prepared to let him step into that opening.

If one man hogs the ball, determined to make every basket, score every point, and claim all the glory, the game will collapse, and everyone will lose out.

Sometimes we have to give up a personal victory for the greater good of our fellow players.

We have to take one for the team.

Two of the most important words in a marriage are we and us. The two words that have destroyed more marriages than any other are I and me.

Certainly, those words have done no such thing, but the attitude behind the words is what stirs up anger, animosity, and division. Eventually, the word divorce comes out, and it creates a rift that can never be undone. It's a scar that rubs us badly every time it reappears.

In Ezra 9:6, we read of the great prophet's confession of sin:

> "Oh, my God, I am ashamed and blush to lift up my face to you, my God: for our iniquities are increased over our head, and our trespass is grown up unto the heavens."

Note the switch in mid text from the personal pronouns I and my to the inclusive pronoun our. What's significant here is that Ezra had committed no sin. His docket was pure and unblemished. Israel, however, had no such claim to purity. They had intermarried with the heathen people around them, thereby polluting the holiness of God's people.

Yet, Ezra was a team player, willing to wrap himself in the wrongdoings of his people and accept that he was responsible by association. He had to take this one for his team, God's chosen people, the children of Israel. When they stumbled, they must be lifted up, and that could only happen when they were lifted up together.

Sometimes our family wrongs us, and we want to thrust our fist into the air and cry, "I did nothing wrong!" Maybe not, but we're a team. It's the word we that matters, not I, me, or my.

Let's take one for the team. We'll bring about a greater victory if we work together than if we try to go it on our own.

Our Christian walk is not about us. It's about all of us.

Light Bulb Moment

Draw nigh unto God, and he will make us into his own image.

Taking Our Hand Off the Sword

WE LOVE to get even.

Take World War II for example. Europe was being ripped apart by the tyranny of Hitler. The other side of the world faced decimation by a virulent Japanese military. The United States stood aloof, refusing to get involved except in the most carefully "uninvolved" manner.

It took an attack on our nation's sovereign soil to invoke our wrath. When Pearl Harbor was hit by the Japanese, we reacted with furor. The indignity was beyond belief. The infamy would not be tolerated. America's great fist swung into motion, and we crushed the two mighty powers that threatened the rest of the world.

We might call it justice, but it felt really good to get

even.

Our criminal justice system is much the same. It's all about the justice, but we also want the victims to feel satisfied with the sentence meted out. If the criminal gets off on a technicality, we feel cheated and hollow, as if we've been betrayed by a court system that's let us down.

How do we feel about spiritual injustice? The Bible takes a stand on the matter in Romans 12:19:

> "Beloved, never avenge yourselves, but leave it to the wrath of God, for it is written, 'Vengeance is mine, I will repay, says the Lord.' "

Our neighbor maligns us, creating fractious relationships in our neighborhood. Do we spread vicious rumors about them, or do we smile and speak of the goodness of the Lord?

Our spouse abandons us for greener pastures. Do we use our children as weapons to punish him or her? Or do we leave it in the hands of our almighty God for the greater good of our children's well-being?

We feel slighted by our choir director, as she chooses less skilled soloists each Sunday morning. Do we make snide comments, even skip Wednesday night practices, just to make our point clear? Or do we raise our hands in praise anyway, trusting the Father to work his grace through every song, no matter whose voice sings it?

Getting even is not in God's dictates for our lives. We will feel wronged. That's the nature of living with our fellow human beings. The nature of living with our Father God is to show forgiveness, for that is the Christ-like thing to do.

Draw nigh unto God, and he will make us into his own image.

Light Bulb Moment

When we stand shoulder-to-shoulder with our fellow Christians, we become stronger than we were before.

The Bricks We Stand On

BRICK FOUNDATIONS. They look good, and they work very well.

Most importantly, a good brick foundation lifts our house above the surrounding soil. Termites can't reach our wood superstructure. Rising water can flow right past us. Building on a solid brick foundation is the only way to construct our lives.

1 Thessalonians 5:11 tells us:

> "Therefore encourage one another and build one another up, just as you are doing."

Our fellow Christians are the bricks that make up our foundations in Christ. They are placed in our lives one brick at a time, one friendly greeting at a time, and one Sunday lunch at a time. Throw a Super Bowl party, invite our Sunday school class, and believe it or not, we'll become more closely bonded to our fellow Christians, becoming bricks firmly wedged under each other to support our Christian walk when the water begins to rise around us.

Here's what the Bible says about laying our brick foundations.

James 1:27 tells us what our bricks are made of.

> "Religion that is pure and undefiled before God, the Father, is this: to visit orphans and widows in their affliction, and to keep oneself unstained from the world."

Our bricks must be of the highest quality. Otherwise, they will crumble in times of stress. We are lifting up other people. They depend on us to support them in their times of need. We cannot afford to be weak in our walk with Christ.

Luke 10:27 gives us the mortar that holds our bricks one against another:

> "And he answered, 'You shall love the Lord your God with all your heart and with all your soul and with all your strength and with all your mind, and your neighbor as yourself.' "

One brick isn't enough to build a good foundation. Even a truckload just dumped on the ground will be no more than a pile of bricks. Stack them without mortar, and the slightest push will knock the over. Our bricks must be solid, and our mortar must be of the very best quality. Then our lives will withstand the harshest of weather, and we will come through every time.

When we stand shoulder-to-shoulder with our fellow Christians, we become stronger than we were before.

Light Bulb Moment

When we step in to help our fellow believers,
God reaches down and does the rest.

The Helpful Nephew

PAUL OF NEW Testament fame was a family man.

Oh, be assured, he wasn't married. Nor did he have children, but there was a family. Thank God there was a family.

The Jews of Paul's day vilified him. Just as with Jesus, they felt threatened by the message of the Christ. Rather than glory in the coming of their promised king, the Jews were up in arms, worried that their power structure would be toppled; and they were determined to root out any threat to their social standing and their perceived positions of authority.

They wanted Paul destroyed.

Yet, Paul was a family man, and he had people who cared about him. Acts 23:16 reveals the moment of supreme familial love:

> "And when Paul's sister's son heard of their lying in wait, he went and entered into the castle and told Paul."

There was an element of risk in what Paul's nephew did. He could have been accused of involvement in the Jew's plot to kill his uncle. He could have been arrested, even retained in custody along with Paul. After all, he was a Jew, also.

Paul trusted God, and Verse 17 reveals Paul's response:

> "Then Paul called one of the centurions unto him, and said, Bring this young man unto the chief captain: for he has a certain thing to say."

The chief captain's response was to give Paul an escort of two hundred soldiers along with seventy horsemen and two hundred spearmen.

An escort of nearly 500 men, all because of Paul's nephew.

Are we family men and women in today's church? Are we willing to take a risk for those we call father, mother, uncle, aunt, and nephew? Do we consider our brothers and sisters in Christ to be worth our time and effort?

If they are about to be ambushed, are we willing to step in and accept a measure of risk to keep them safe?

Are we a helpful nephew?

We will be, if we follow in the way of Christ.

When we step in to help our fellow believers, God reaches down and does the rest.

Light Bulb Moment

A spiritual superhero is one who follows the example of Jesus and places the welfare of others first in everything they do.

The Sons of Thunder

SUPERHERO MOVIES are all the rage right now. Drive by any theater and read the marquee. We'll see the names of Superman, Thor, and the Green Hornet; all the Marvel characters and more that have personas bigger than life.

These are characters that can crush cars with a mighty green fist, turn into impervious stone, become invisible at will, and fly through the skies simply because they wish it. Yet, even as we enjoy the feats that flash across the big screen, we accept the lack of reality that makes it all possible. No one can really raise a hammer and make thunder reverberate across the heavens.

Or can they?

Two men became the superheroes of Jesus' time. They rocked their world. They were filled with impetuous attitudes and spouted zeal in everything they did.

Nothing could slow them down.

They raised their fists, and bam! Down went the enemy. They stepped into any situation, no matter how dire, and they took control.

No one wanted to mess with the Sons of Thunder.

Jesus enjoyed the Sons of Thunder so much that he renamed them Boanerges (which means sons of thunder). Jesus truly found pleasure in these two men.

Read of it in Mark 3:17:

> "And James the son of Zebedee, and John the brother of James; and [Jesus] surnamed them Boanerges, which is, The sons of thunder."

What superhero qualities do we have? What does Jesus see in us that tempts him to give us a new name? Would he rename us Encourager? Prayer Warrior? Faithful Servant?

Or would he give us a lesser name? Not all those who wield superpowers are admirable. No one wants to be a Joker, a villain who is twisted beyond all that is good and honorable.

If we want to know how Jesus sees us, we need to ask those around us. Have each person we know write down a good quality they see in us. Collect the answers, and our superhero will begin to emerge.

Maybe Jesus sees us as Sons of Thunder after all.

A spiritual superhero is one who follows the example of Jesus and places the welfare of others first in everything they do.

Light Bulb Moment

When we care about other people, we place them above us in our prayers, actions, and honor.

The Value of a Little Man

SO, WHO'S the little guy in our life? Is it the boy down the street who's just learning to ride his bike, or how about the new office employee who's stepped into an entry-level position?

It's the totem pole thing . . . who's on top, and who's on bottom. Our totem can represent anything: age; experience; finances; health.

Even our relationship with Christ can take on a totem pole-like appearance, with cardinals, bishops, and the lowly laity, each showing up at different stations for prayers on Sunday morning.

Where do our servants fit into this totem pole? Several decades ago, a British comedy came out called *Upstairs, Downstairs*. It illustrated the differences between the lives of the wealthy in the main portion of the house, and the servants in the kitchen downstairs. More recently, many of us are familiar with *Downton Abbey*. In this version, the aristocrats in the manor have a vested interest in the servants living beneath their feet, and they treat them very much as family.

The people they depend on to maintain their lives and keep their house functioning in an orderly fashion have become important to them, and when their servants hurt, their masters hurt with them.

Matthew 8:5-6 tells the story of the centurion with a suffering servant.

> "When [Jesus] entered Capernaum, a centurion came forward to him, appealing to him, 'Lord, my servant is lying paralyzed at home, suffering terribly.' "

The central part of this story lies not in the healing, although Jesus certainly did that for the centurion, but rather, let's bring out the centurion's willingness to appeal to Jesus in the first place. The centurion didn't come in power and might, placing a demand simply because it was his right. He came pleading for healing, not for himself, but for a servant he cared deeply about.

Matthew 8:8 paints a picture of the centurion's humble spirit.

"The centurion replied, 'Lord, I am not worthy to have you come under my roof, but only say the word, and my servant will be healed.'"

How do we treat the little guy we associate with every day? The lawn man, do we greet him as an equal, or as a nuisance? How about the cashier at the grocery store, or the woman pushing a broom at the big box store? Or do we just see a little man, one who's not our equal and not worth a little bit of our day?

Next time we're out to eat, have a meaningful conversation with the waitress. It may only be two sentences, but it might make the difference in her having a miserable day and the best day of her life.

When we care about other people, we place them above us in our prayers, actions, and honor.

Light Bulb Moment

When life doesn't give us what we want, we must remember that God is the master at bringing forth something out of nothing.

The Yin Pollutes the Yang

OPPOSITES. They make the world function as it should.

Take two magnets, put the opposing poles together, and we can create an electric motor.

Male and female did God make the creatures of all the earth.

Without the night, the day would never return. We would fry in the blast of eternal sunshine (and get very sleepy, too).

Yin and Yang is an Oriental concept that illustrates the opposing forces of life. Everything is a balance of opposites. If we have this, we must expect that.

Yet, in a garden, if we allow the weeds to grow up with the good plants, they will suck the nutrients out of the soil, and our crops will suffer as they mature. We want one without the other.

Yin without yang.

Matthew 13:26 falls in the midst of a parable about the gospel of Christ. Jesus uses something very familiar to his disciples to illustrate the point he's making.

Jesus speaks about planting crops.

> "But when the blade was sprung up, and brought forth fruit, then appeared the tares also."

Yin and yang. It's in our churches, our relationships, and scattered throughout our walk with Christ. Opposites. It's to be expected.

Jesus didn't say to yank the tares out, either. In Verse 30, he cautions:

> "Let both grow together until the harvest [at which time] gather the wheat into my barn."

Only God has the wisdom and ability to accurately decide which is the good blade, and which is the tare. In our enthusiasm, we might very well pull God's seedling from the ground, and it will die in the field rather than producing a good crop for him.

It's the reason why factions are tolerated within the body of Christ. Along with the tares we find the good plants, and they will bring forth good fruit for the kingdom.

Let's leave the weeding up to him.

When life doesn't give us what we want, we must remember that God is the master at bringing forth something out of nothing.

Light Bulb Moment

The whole is as strong as the one. We must be pillars of strength for Christ.

Threading the Needle of Christ

A TAPESTRY is a painting in thread.

As we create our thread painting on our loom, there are four vital things we must consider.

First, our loom must be dedicated. It will be used for one painting until it is completely finished. The threads that are woven into the final picture cannot be removed and replaced at will without destroying our finished work.

Second, we need a beater. It can be wood, metal, or a combination. The construction isn't important. What counts is how well it presses the threads into position to ensure a compact and well-formed final product.

Third, the warp (thread) must be very strong. It will

be under extreme tension during the weaving process. If we can break it easily with our hands, it will fail us before we are done.

Fourth, the threads we weave into our image must disappear into the overall tapestry. The beginnings and ends will be skillfully hidden, with people unable to detect the individual strands.

1 Timothy 2:9 tells us:

> "Women should adorn themselves in respectable apparel, with modesty and self-control, not with braided hair and gold or pearls or costly attire."

Yet Ezekiel 16:10 says:

> "I clothed you also with embroidered cloth and shod you with fine leather. I wrapped you in fine linen and covered you with silk."

So what do we do? Are we to be somber and staid, or should we endeavor to shine with the best the world has to offer?

We need to look back at our tapestry.

We must be dedicated. Christ is our only purpose.

He is the needle that weaves us into the church, placing us just where we need to be to create the best effect in the final image.

We will be in close contact with those around us. Our walk with Christ will force us to rub shoulders with our fellow Christians, and we will become one with them.

Strength of character is vital. Impurities, no matter how fuzzy, warm, or entreating to our carnal minds, will cause the church to fail when put under stress.

We are not the final product. The work of Christ on earth and his message of the cross are all people should be able to see in us.

The story in Ezekiel tells of a faithless church that began to see herself as beautiful because of her fine jewels and great beauty. She forgot she was one thread in a vast tapestry, and she lost herself to the world. She failed when put under stress, because warm and fuzzy was more important than strength of character.

We need to consider that we are the threads woven with the needle of Christ. We need to be beautiful for him. However, do we make the church stronger? Or will we fail him when he needs us most? If all we care about is appearance, we've become a weak thread in the tapestry of the church. Just like with any project woven in thread, if one part fails, the rest becomes useless, also.

Let's make our threads strong, so that the church will remain strong as well.

The whole is as strong as the one. We must be pillars of strength for Christ.

Light Bulb Moment

Let's work our chores around the people we love, not work the people we love around our chores.

Unimportant Matters

A SPLINTER in a child's fingers.

On the scale of world events, that splinter doesn't matter even the smallest amount. There are starving children in Third-World countries with distended bellies whose only wish is for a bite of food. They wouldn't notice something as small as a sliver of wood penetrating the skin.

Yet when pierced by pain, that splinter becomes the child's world. There is no disaster greater, and our hearts are broken by the tears we see running down that tender face. What seems unimportant to the world is everything to that child, and our hearts are broken in response. That splinter matters more than we can say, and we set everything aside to make it right.

What seems unimportant to the world matters to a tender heart.

Luke tells us the story of Martha and Mary. Sisters, they nevertheless held different mindsets. One was focused on the necessities of everyday living, and the other was focused on the necessities of the heart. In Luke 10:40, at a crisis of contention, Martha wails her dismay to Jesus.

> "But Martha was cumbered about much serving, and came to him, and said, Lord, do you not care that my sister has left me to serve alone? Bid her therefore that she help me."

Mary was at Jesus' feet soaking in his teaching. To Martha, her sister was wasting her time when she had better things to do. Mary was taken up with unimportant matters, when there were chores to be done.

Jesus saw things differently. What's unimportant to the unchurched and unsaved are the very matters we need to pay attention to: the teachings of Christ; love for our fellow man; and the worship of our almighty God. If the necessities of everyday living are left undone, and we focus on the necessities of the heart, then we've found what matters most in our relationship with God and with our fellow man.

It's the seemingly unimportant matters that matter

most when we have the opportunity to kneel at Jesus' feet. Every day we are given a choice we must make. Kneel in prayer, or scrub the floor one extra time. Read in our Bible, or complete that extra report for our job. Bake a cake to share with our neighbor, or store up an extra few dollars in the cookie jar.

What are the important things that really matter? We must weigh our choices, because we are the ones that get to choose.

Let's work our chores around the people we love, not work the people we love around our chores.

Coming to Christ
In Three Easy Steps

If you do not know Christ as your personal savior, there is no better time than the present to turn your life over to him.

- Step 1 is to admit that you are human, God is God, and you need his grace.
- Step 2 is to place your belief in him. You must accept that he is the Son of the Eternal God, and through his death on the cross, he can give you new life.
- Step 3 is to turn from your previous ways and receive the hope of Jesus' power in you.

Fill in the following information as a testament to your decision to accept Jesus as your Savior.

I, _____, accept Jesus
            print your full name

as my personal savior on _____.
                               today's date

_____
            your signature

Look for these additional topics on the MyChurchNotes.net website:

2 Timothy
Beatitudes
Discipleship
Evangelism
Faith
Family
Healing
Hope
Kingdom of God
Money
Prayer
Relationships
Repentance
Salvation
Worship

MyChurchNotes.net is a faith-based ministry founded on a belief in the Father, the Son, and the Holy Spirit. All MyChurchNotes.net articles are based on Scripture and created especially for MyChurchNotes.net.

Our Mission Statement is to take the Word of God into all the nations, and proclaim that he is Lord!

If you enjoyed
God Renews Our Relationships with Others,
please visit us at our website:

www.MyChurchNotes.net
and
www.MyChurchNotes.com

We look forward to hearing from you.

Website and Publication Powered by:

Bright Herd . . . for All Your Website and Media Design Needs.
www.brightherd.com
contact@brightherd.com

www.ingramcontent.com/pod-product-compliance
Lightning Source LLC
LaVergne TN
LVHW051833080426
835512LV00018B/2859